★
ICONS

MOROCCO STYLE

MOROCC

Exteriors Interiors

O STYLE

Details

AUTHOR **Christiane Reiter**
EDITOR **Angelika Taschen**

TASCHEN

KÖLN LONDON LOS ANGELES MADRID PARIS TOKYO

Front cover:
Today, a king: place of honour at the pool of a riyad in Marrakech.
Photo: René Stoeltie
Back cover:
Take a seat: easy chair behind a highly decorative door in Marrakech.
Foto: René Stoeltie

Couverture :
Etre roi pour un jour : place d'honneur sur le bassin d'un riad à Marrakech.
Photo : René Stoeltie
Dos de couverture :
Invitation à prendre place : fauteuil derrière une porte richement décorée à Marrakech.
Photo : René Stoeltie

Umschlagvorderseite:
Heute ein König: Ehrenplatz am Pool eines Riad in Marrakesch.
Foto: René Stoeltie
Umschlagrückseite:
Nehmen Sie Platz: Sessel hinter einer reich verzierten Tür in Marrakesch.
Foto: René Stoeltie

Also available from TASCHEN:

Living in Morocco
280 pages
3–8228–1383–4 (English/French/German)
3–8228–1352–4 (edition with French cover)

To stay informed about upcoming TASCHEN titles, please request our magazine
at www.taschen.com or write to TASCHEN, Hohenzollernring 53, D-50672 Cologne,
Germany, Fax: +49-221-254919. We will be happy to send you a free copy
of our magazine which is filled with information about all of our books.

© 2004 TASCHEN GmbH
Hohenzollernring 53, D-50672 Köln
www.taschen.com

Concept by Angelika Taschen, Berlin
Layout and general project management by Stephanie Bischoff, Cologne
Texts by Christiane Reiter, Berlin
Lithography by Horst Neuzner, Cologne
English translation by Pauline Cumbers, Frankfurt/Main
French translation by Thérèse Chatelain-Südkamp, Cologne

Printed in Italy
ISBN 3–8228–3463–7

CONTENTS SOMMAIRE INHALT

Although separated from Europe only by the narrow Straits of Gibraltar, Morocco is already another world: an exotic kingdom, an oriental fairy-tale country, a desert state full of adventurous promise. Here more than anywhere else, the cliché of those opposites that attract is alive and well. Often only a few kilometres separate palaces fit for Arabian Nights from Berber villages built of sun-blanched mud. Souks that exude the magic of the Orient are surrounded by modern city quarters with a slightly seedy charm. The snow-capped Atlas mountains sparkle behind the palm groves, and behind the sweeping sand-dunes the Atlantic.

Yet however different Morocco's faces are, there is something they have in common: a beauty that seems to hover somewhere between seduction and decay.

THE MAGIC OF MOROCCO
Christiane Reiter

Royaume exotique sorti tout droit d'un conte de fées oriental, contrée désertique prometteuse d'aventures, on se sent tout de suite dépaysé au Maroc même si seul le détroit de Gibraltar le sépare de l'Europe. Rares sont les endroits où s'épanouissent d'aussi riches contrastes. Souvent les palais des Mille et Une Nuits ne sont qu'à quelques kilomètres des villages berbères avec leurs maisons de torchis décolorées par le soleil. Tout autour des souks au charme oriental s'étendent les quartiers modernes ; au-delà des palmeraies scintillent les sommets neigeux de l'Atlas et derrière les immenses dunes aux courbes douces on peut apercevoir l'Atlantique.

Pourtant tous ces visages du Maroc, aussi différents soient-ils, ont un point commun : une beauté à mi-chemin entre la séduction et le déclin. Architectes et designers du monde entier

Nur durch die schmale Straße von Gibraltar von Europa getrennt, ist Marokko doch bereits eine andere Welt: ein exotisches Königreich, ein orientalisches Märchenland, ein Abenteuer versprechender Wüstenstaat. Und so lebendig wie an kaum einem anderen Ort ist hier das Klischee von sich anziehenden Gegensätzen. Zwischen Palästen wie aus 1001 Nacht und Berberdörfern aus sonnengebleichtem Lehm liegen oft nur wenige Kilometer, rund um Souks mit dem Zauber des Orients klammern sich moderne Stadtviertel mit leicht ver-ruchtem Charme, man sieht hinter Palmenhainen die schnee-bedeckten Atlasgipfel blitzen und hinter weit geschwungenen Dünen den Atlantik.

Doch so unterschiedlich die Gesichter Marokkos auch sind, eines haben sie gemeinsam: eine Schönheit, die auf dem Grat

Architects and designers from all over the world have fallen in love with that beauty and been inspired by it. They have combined traditional crafts and modern stylistic elements to create surprise-laden dream houses out of ramshackle properties. Unadorned doors conceal colourful mosaics, filigree cedarwood arches or fountains strewn with rose-petals. Plain wooden doors open onto rooms full of velvet and silk. Simple brass dishes reflect on brightly distempered walls or add the finishing touch to a completely white room. This captivating blend of old culture preserved and own creativity discovered is the magic of Morocco.

sont tombés amoureux de cette beauté et s'en inspirent. L'artisanat traditionnel se voit combiné à des éléments stylistiques modernes et des maisons de rêve étonnantes retrouvent une seconde jeunesse à partir de bâtiments délabrés. Derrière des portes dénuées de tout ornement, le visiteur surpris découvre des mosaïques colorées, des arcs en bois de cèdre sculptés comme de la dentelle ou des fontaines dont les bassins sont parsemés de pétales de rose. Des portes en bois toutes simples s'ouvrent sur des pièces où s'amassent la soie et le satin ; des coupes en laiton aux lignes sobres jettent des lueurs ensoleillées sur les murs badigeonnés de couleur ou confèrent une élégance suprême à une pièce immaculée. C'est un mélange fascinant de culture traditionnelle et de créativité personnelle – c'est la magie du Maroc.

zwischen Verführung und Verfall zu balancieren scheint. In sie haben sich Architekten und Designer aus aller Welt verliebt und lassen sich von ihr inspirieren. Da werden traditionelle Handwerkskünste mit modernen Stilelementen verbunden und aus maroden Anwesen Traumhäuser voller Überraschungen geschaffen. Hinter schmucklosen Türen verbergen sich bunte Mosaike, filigrane Zedernholzbögen oder Brunnen, in deren Becken Rosenblätter schweben. Einfache Holztüren öffnen sich zu Zimmern voller Samt und Seide, schlichte Messingschalen werfen ihren Glanz auf bunt getünchte Wände oder verleihen einem Raum in Weiß den letzten Schliff. Es ist eine faszinierende Mischung aus dem Bewahren alter Kultur und dem Entdecken eigener Kreativität – es ist die Magie Marokkos.

"…wide transparent space spreads out over me and on the horizon its iridescent blue fades into a light sea-green. Everything is bright, radiant, a magic feast of light!…"

Pierre Loti, in: *Au Maroc*

«…un vide immense, profond, limpide, qui est ce soir d'un bleu irisé, d'un bleu tournant, à l'horizon, au vert d'aigue-marine; il y a partout grand resplendissement, grande fête et grande magie de lumière!…»

Pierre Loti, dans: *Au Maroc*

»…Ein weiter, durchsichtiger Raum dehnt sich über mir und sein irisierendes Blau verglimmert am Horizont in lichtes Meergrün. Alles leuchtet, alles strahlt, ein Zauberfest des Lichts!…«

Pierre Loti, in: *Im Zeichen der* Sahara

EXTERIORS

Extérieurs Außenwelten

10/11 Climbing course: goats on a nut tree near Essaouira. *Escalade : chèvres sur un noyer près d'Essaouira.* Kletterkurs: Ziegen auf einem Nussbaum bei Essaouira.
Photo: René Stoeltie

12/13 Tall and slender: grove in the elegant district of La Palmeraie. *Des arbres majestueux : dans le quartier chic de La Palmeraie à Marrakech.* Hoch gewachsen: Hain im Nobelviertel La Palmeraie.
Photo: René Stoeltie

14/15 Behind high walls: the Palais Jamaï hotel in Fez. *Protégé par de hauts murs : le palais transformé en hôtel « Palais Jamaï » à Fès.* Hinter hohen Mauern: Das Palasthotel Palais Jamaï in Fes.
Photo: Guy Hervais

16/17 Like a bastion on the sea: the old town of Essaouira. *Place forte sur la mer : la vieille ville d'Essaouira.* Wie eine Trutzburg am Meer: Essaouiras Altstadt.
Photo: René Stoeltie

18/19 Over the roofs of Marrakech: on the terrace of Riad Enija. *Sur les toits de Marrakech: la terrasse du Riad Enija.* Über den Dächern von Marrakesch: Auf der Terrasse des Riad Enija.
Photo: Reto Guntli

20/21 Reflected in water: Hotel Amanjena near Marrakech. *Se reflète dans l'eau : l'hôtel Amanjena près de Marrakech.* Im Wasser gespiegelt: Das Hotel Amanjena bei Marrakesch.
Photo: René Stoeltie

22/23 White-blue paradise: the Maison des Artistes in Essaouira. *Paradis en bleu et blanc : la Maison des Artistes à Essaouira.* Weiß-blaues Paradies: Die Maison des Artistes in Essaouira.
Photo: Reto Guntli

24/25 New perspectives: view of the sky above Morocco. *Nouvelles perspectives : le ciel du Maroc.* Neue Perspektiven: Blick in den Himmel über Marokko.
Photo: Giulio Oriani/Vega MG

26/27 Dining area: in the garden of the little house La Folie in Tangier. *Coin repas : dans le jardin de la maison La Folie à Tanger.* Essecke: Im Garten des Häuschens La Folie in Tanger.
Photo: René Stoeltie

28/29 Sun sails: on the veranda of the Dar El Qadi hotel in Marrakech. *Voilure de soleil : sur la véranda de l'hôtel Dar El Qadi à Marrakech.* Sonnensegel: Auf der Veranda des Hotels Dar El Qadi in Marrakesch.
Photo : Giulio Oriani/Vega MG

30/31 Luxury camping site: in the courtyard of a house in Marrakech. *Des tentes luxueuses : dans la cour d'une maison à Marrakech.* Zelten auf luxuriöse Art: Im Hof eines Hauses in Marrakesch.
Photo: Giulio Oriani/Vega MG

32/33 Shady corner: the patio of Casa Roberto. *Bien ombragé : le patio de la Casa Roberto.* Schön schattig: Der Patio der Casa Roberto.
Photo: Giulio Oriani/Vega MG

34/35 Like a private palace: in front of Philippe Cluzel's house. *Comme un palais privé : devant la maison de Philippe Cluzel.* Wie ein privater Palast: Vor dem Haus von Philippe Cluzel. *Photo: Giulio Oriani/Vega MG*

36/37 Inviting: patio full of nooks and crannies in Marrakech. *Coins et recoins : le patio d'une maison à Marrakech.* Einladend: Verwinkelter Patio eines Hauses in Marrakesch. *Photo: Giulio Oriani/Vega MG*

38/39 A touch of the tropics in town: the Riad Enija von Marrakech. *Ambiance tropicale dans la ville : le Riad Enija de Marrakech.* Tropenflair mitten in der Stadt: Der Riad Enija von Marrakesch. *Photo: Reto Guntli*

40/41 Blossom time: view of the bewitching inner courtyard of the Riad Enija. *Floraison : vue d'une cour intérieure du Riad Enija.* Blütezeit: Blick in den verwunschenen Innenhof des Riad Enija. *Photo: Nicolas Bruant/The Interior Archive*

42/43 Purist: white, grey and green shades in the courtyard of Dar Kawa. *Puriste : tons de blanc, gris et vert dans la cour du Dar Kawa.* Puristisch: Weiß-, Grau- und Grüntöne im Hof des Dar Kawa. *Photo: René Stoeltie*

44/45 Three shades of blue: in front of a Moroccan house. *Trois teintes de bleu : devant une maison d'habitation marocaine.* Drei Farben Blau: Vor einem marokkanischen Wohnhaus. *Photo: Gianni Basso/Vega MG*

46/47 Together: at the private pool of the CaravanSerai hotel near Marrakech. *Vie à deux : piscine privée de l'hôtel CaravanSerai près de Marrakech.* Zweisamkeit: Am Privatpool des Hotels CaravanSerai bei Marrakesch. *Photo: Dorothea Resch*

48/49 Waiting patiently: a melon-seller on the road to the Ourika valley. *En attendant le client : vendeur de melon sur la route menant à la vallée d'Ourika.* Geduldig wartend: Ein Melonenverkäufer an der Straße zum Ourika-Tal. *Photo: René Stoeltie*

50/51 Open doors: Hugo Curletto's house in Marrakech. *Des portes toujours ouvertes : la maison de Hugo Curletto à Marrakech.* Stets offene Türen: Das Haus von Hugo Curletto in Marrakesch. *Photo: René Stoeltie*

52/53 Pure symmetry: patio of the Riad Enija in Marrakech. *Pure symétrie : le patio du Riad Enija à Marrakech.* Reinste Symmetrie: Patio des Riad Enija in Marrakesch. *Photo: Reto Guntli*

54/55 Well thought-out: on the patio of Casa Roberto. *Bien pensé : le patio de la Casa Roberto.* Um die Ecke gedacht: Im Patio der Casa Roberto. *Photo: Giulio Oriani/Vega MG*

56/57 In the shimmering light: evening at the CaravanSerai. *Dans la lueur des éclairages : ambiance nocturne au CaravanSerai.* Im Schein der Lichter: Abendstimmung im CaravanSerai. *Photo: Dorothea Resch*

"…When you opened the door you encountered a whole range of blues: indigo blue in the hallway, sky blue in the inner courtyard, the kitchen, including the brush, was turquoise; when you entered the rooms you were inundated by the sea; at night you stood in a field of forget-me-not…"

Driss Chraibi, dans: *La civilisation, ma mère !*

«…En ouvrant la porte, on était accueilli par toute une palette de bleus : le bleu indigo dans le couloir, le bleu ciel dans la cour intérieure, la cuisine était turquoise, y compris les balais. Quand on pénétrait dans les pièces, on était baigné par la mer, il faisait nuit, on se tenait dans un champ de myosotis…»

Driss Chraibi, dans: *La civilisation, ma mère !*

»…Öffnete man die Tür, empfing einen eine ganze Skala in Blau: Indigo-Blau im Flur, Himmelblau im Innenhof, die Küche war türkis, Besen inbegriffen; betrat man die Zimmer, umspülte einen das Meer, wurde es Nacht, stand man in einem Feld von Vergissmeinnicht…«

Driss Chraibi, in: *Die Zivilisation, Mutter!*

INTERIORS

Intérieurs Innenwelten

62/63 Mighty arches: entrance area of the Amanjena hotel near Marrakech. *Sous des arcs imposants : l'entrée de l'hôtel Amanjena.* Unter mächtigen Bögen: Der Eingangsbereich des Hotels Amanjena.
Photo: René Stoeltie

64/65 Focal point: the bar of Amanjena, with fireplace and round bench. *Le point central : le bar de l'Amanjena avec sa cheminée et son banc circulaire.* Mittelpunkt: Die Bar des Amanjena mit Kamin und Rundbank.
Photo: René Stoeltie

66/67 Touches of red: the living room in Elie Mouyal's country home. *Accents de rouge : dans le salon de la maison de campagne d'Elie Mouyal.* Rote Akzente: Im Salon des Land-hauses von Elie Mouyal.
Photo: René Stoeltie

68/69 Traditional decor: Elie Mouyal's kitchen is decorated with tiles. *Décor traditionnel : la cuisine décorée de carreaux d'Elie Mouyal.* Traditionelles Dekor: Die mit Kacheln verzierte Küche von Elie Mouyal.
Photo: René Stoeltie

70/71 Moroccan mix: in Elie Mouyal's bed-room. *Mélange de dessins marocains : dans la chambre d'Elie Mouyal.* Marrokanischer Mustermix: In Elie Mouyals Schlafzimmer.
Photo: René Stoeltie

72/73 Ethno-style fireplace: Alessandra Lippi-ni's works. *Coin cheminée de style ethnique : œuvres d'Alessandra Lippini.* Kaminecke im Ethno-Stil: Alessandra Lippinis Werke.
Photo: René Stoeltie

74/75 Memories of India: the fireplace of the interior designer Bill Willis. *Souvenir d'Inde : la cheminée du décorateur Bill Willis.* Erinnerung an Indien: Am Kamin des Innenarchitekten Bill Willis.
Photo: René Stoeltie

76/77 Like in The Arabian Nights: sleeping quarters at the Palais Ayadi. *Comme dans les Mille et Une Nuits : chambre à coucher au Palais Ayadi.* Wie aus 1001 Nacht: Schlaf-gemach im Palais Ayadi.
Photo: René Stoeltie

78/79 Think pink: the stylist Hugo Curletto's house in Marrakech. *La vie en rose: dans la maison du styliste Hugo Curletto à Marrakech.* Think Pink: Im Haus des Stylisten Hugo Curletto in Marrakesch.
Photo: René Stoeltie

80/81 Threads of gold: relaxing on cushions at Palais Ayadi. *Brochés de fils d'or : se détendre sur les canapés du Palais Ayadi.* Golddurchwirkt: Entspannen auf den Polstern des Palais Ayadi.
Photo: René Stoeltie

82/83 Decorative items: original tiles and a modern lamp by Hugo Curletto. *De véritables petits trésors : les carreaux d'origine et la lampe moderne chez Hugo Curletto.* Schmuckstücke: Originale Fliesen und moderne Lampe bei Hugo Curletto. *Photo: René Stoeltie*

84/85 Skilfully restored: smoking room at Frans Ankoné's home. *Restauré d'une main de maître : le salon fumoir chez Frans Ankoné.* Meisterhaft restauriert: Herrenzimmer bei Frans Ankoné.
Photo: René Stoeltie

86/87 Turquoise dream:guestroom with a gold sickle above the fireplace. *Un rêve de turquoise : la chambre d'amis avec une serpe en or au-dessus de la cheminée.* Traum in Türkis: Gästezimmer mit Goldsichel über dem Kamin. *Photo: René Stoeltie*

88/89 Like a twinkling starry sky: sleeping quarters at Frans Ankoné's house. *Comme un ciel étoilé : la chambre à coucher de Frans Ankoné.* Wie ein funkelnder Sternenhimmel: Schlafgemach bei Frans Ankoné.
Photo: René Stoeltie

90/91 Homage to the Ottoman Empire: the gallery of Riad El Cadi. *Hommage au royaume ottoman : la galerie du Riad El Cadi.* Hommage ans osmanische Reich: Die Galerie des Riad El Cadi.
Photo: René Stoeltie

92/93 Green nuances: Marie-Jo Lafontaine's bedroom in Marrakech. *Nuances de vert: la chambre à coucher de Marie-Jo Lafontaine à Marrakech.* Nuancen in Grün: Das Schlafzimmer von Marie-Jo Lafontaine in Marrakesch.
Photo: René Stoeltie

94/95 Dynamic: red fibreglass chair at Riad El Cadi. *Dynamique : chaise rouge en fibre de verre au Riad El Cadi.* Schwungvoll: Roter Glasfiberstuhl im Riad El Cadi.
Photo: René Stoeltie

96/97 Simple elegance: Marie-Jo Lafontaine's living-room. *Elégance sobre : le séjour de Marie-Jo Lafontaine.* Schlichte Eleganz: Das Wohnzimmer von Marie-Jo Lafontaine
Photo: René Stoeltie

98/99 Ample space and peace: at the Riad Enija hotel in Marrakech. *Beaucoup d'espace et de calme : à l'hôtel Riad Enija à Marrakech.* Viel Raum und Ruhe: Im Hotel Riad Enija in Marrakesch.
Photo: Nicolas Bruant/The Interior Archive

100/101 Artful four-poster bed: lilac-coloured bedroom in the Riad Enija. *Un lit à baldaquin comme œuvre d'art : chambre à coucher lilas au Riad Enija.* Himmelbett als Kunstwerk: Fliederfarbenes Schlafzimmer im Riad Enija.
Photo: Nicolas Bruant/The Interior Archive

102/103 Seated on flowers: in a traditional living-room in the Ourika valley. *Etre assis sur des fleurs : dans une salle de séjour traditionnelle de la vallée d'Ourika.* Auf Blumen sitzen: In einem traditionellen Wohnzimmer in Ourika-Tal. *Photo: René Stoeltie*

104/105 Going up: staircase in the Casa Roberto. *Vers les hauteurs : l'escalier de la Casa Roberto.* Auf dem Weg nach oben: Treppenhaus der Casa Roberto.
Photo: Giulio Oriani/Vega MG

106/107 Mirror on the wall: bedroom at the Casa Roberto. *Miroir, joli miroir : chambre à coucher dans la Casa Roberto.* Spieglein an der Wand: Schlafzimmer in der Casa Roberto.
Photo: Giulio Oriani/Vega MG

108/109 Behind twin doors: a living-room at the Casa Roberto. *Derrière des portes jumelles : une pièce de la Casa Roberto.* Hinter Zwillingstüren: Ein Wohnraum der Casa Roberto.
Photo: Giulio Oriani/Vega MG

110/111 Just sink in: plush sofa at the Riad Enija. *Invitation à se prélasser : le sofa en peluche du Riad Enija.* Zum Hineinsinken: Plüschiges Sofa im Riad Enija.
Photo: Reto Guntli

112/113 Art in the bathroom: at the Maison des Artistes in Essaouira. *De l'art dans la salle de bains : dans la Maison des Artistes à Essaouira.* Kunst im Bad: In der Maison des Artistes in Essaouira.
Photo: Reto Guntli

114/115 Under bright blankets: the Maison des Artistes. *Des plafonds clairs : la Maison des Artistes.* Unter hellen Decken: Die Maison des Artistes.
Photo: Reto Guntli

116/117 Attractive conglomeration: at the Maison des Artistes. *Mélange disparate bien sympathique : dans la Maison des Artistes.* Sympathisches Sammelsurium: In der Maison des Artistes.
Photo: Reto Guntli

118/119 Gentle sunlight: bedroom at the Maison des Artistes. *Caressée par les rayons du soleil : chambre à coucher de la Maison des Artistes.* Im sanften Sonnenschein: Schlafzimmer der Maison des Artistes.
Photo: Reto Guntli

120/121 Dinner for six: dining-room of a house in Marrakech. *Place pour six personnes : salle à manger d'une maison de Marrakech.* Platz für sechs Personen: Esszimmer eines Hauses in Marrakesch.
Photo: Reto Guntli

122/123 The opposite of kitsch: simple bedroom in Marrakech. *Absence de kitsch : la sobriété d'une chambre à coucher de Marrakech.* Kein Kitsch: Schlichtes Schlafzimmer in Marrakesch.
Photo: Giulio Oriani/Vega MG

"…Everywhere, on walls, beside doors, at some distance from the floor, were painted big hands, each finger clearly outlined, mostly in blue: as protection against the evil eye…"

Elias Canetti, in: *The voices of Marrakesh*

«…Partout, sur les murs, à côté des portes, à une certaine hauteur du sol, des mains étaient peintes en grand, en suivant exactement le contour des doigts, et la plupart du temps en couleur bleue : ces mains étaient censées conjurer le mauvais œil…»

Elias Canetti, dans: *Les voix de Marrakech*

»…Überall, auf Mauern, neben Türen, in einiger Höhe vom Boden, waren Hände groß aufgemalt, jeder Finger deutlich umrissen, meist in blauer Farbe: Sie galten der Abwehr gegen den bösen Blick…«

Elias Canetti, in: *Die Stimme von Marrakesch*

DETAILS

Détails Details

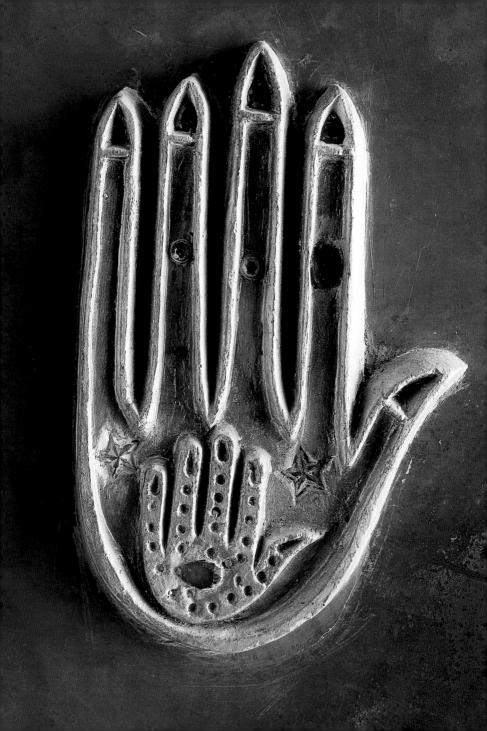

130 Lantern and painting: in a former harem in Marrakech. *Lanterne et peintures : dans un ancien harem de Marrakech.* Laterne und Gemälde: In einem ehemaligen Harem in Marrakesch. *Photo: René Stoeltie*

132 Shell embroidery: at the Amanjena hotel near Marrakech. *Broderie de coquillages : dans l'hôtel Amanjena près de Marrakech.* Muschelstickerei: Im Hotel Amanjena bei Marrakesch. *Photo: René Stoeltie*

133 Sweet-and-sour national dish: tajine with lamb and apricots. *Plat national doux-amer : tagine d'agneau aux abricots.* Süß-saures Nationalgericht: Tajine mit Lamm und Aprikosen. *Photo: René Stoeltie*

134 Supporting cushions: at the Dar El Qadi hotel in Marrakech. *Trois coussins dans le dos : dans l'hôtel Dar El Qadi à Marrakech.* Drei Kissen im Rücken: Im Hotel Dar El Qadi in Marrakesch. *Photo: Giulio Oriani/ Vega MG*

136 Devoted to beauty: at the CaravanSerai hotel. *Voué à la beauté : l'hôtel CaravanSerai.* Dem Schönen verbunden: Im Hotel CaravanSerai. *Photo: Dorothea Resch*

137 Headfirst: flower-strewn sculpture. *Par dessus tête : sculpture décorée de fleur.* Kopfüber: Blütengeschmückte Skulptur. *Photo: Dorothea Resch*

138 View of the sea: at the Maison des Artistes. *Vue sur la mer : dans la Maison des Artistes.* Blick aufs Meer: In der Maison des Artistes. *Photo: Reto Guntli*

140 Trio: traditional Moroccan lanterns. *Trio : lanternes marocaines traditionnelles.* Trio: Traditionelle marokkanische Laternen. *Photo: Giulio Oriani/ Vega MG*

141 Handcraft: arched doorway in Marrakech. *Fait main : arceau à Marrakech.* Handarbeit: Torbogen in Marrakesch. *Photo: Giulio Oriani/ Vega MG*

142 Chair on stripes: at the Maison des Artistes. *Chaise et rayures : dans la Maison des Artistes.* Stuhl auf Streifen: In der Maison des Artistes. *Photo: Reto Guntli*

144 Trophy: buffalo head at the Ministerio del Gusto. *Trophée : tête de buffle au Ministerio del Gusto.* Trophäe: Büffelkopf im Ministerio del Gusto. *Photo: René Stoeltie*

145 Steep stairs: staircase at the Ministerio del Gusto. *Marches raides : escalier au Ministerio del Gusto.* Steile Stufen: Treppenhaus im Ministero del Gusto. *Photo: René Stoeltie*

146 Floating roses: in the inner courtyard of Hugo Curletto's house. *Roses flottantes : dans la cour intérieure de la maison de Hugo Curletto.* Schwimmende Rosen: Im Innenhof von Hugo Curlettos Haus. *Photo: René Stoeltie*

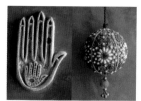

148 Against the evil eye: the hand of Fatima. *Protection contre le mauvais œil : la main de Fatima.* Schutz vor dem bösen Blick: Die Hand der Fatima. *Photo: René Stoeltie*

149 With pearls: lightpull in Frans Ankoné's house. *G'ami de perles : le cordon de l'interrupteur dans la maison de Frans Ankoné.* Mit Perlen: Schalterschnur im Haus von Frans Ankoné. *Photo: René Stoeltie*

150 Sugar sweet: Moroccan almond cookies. *Sucrés : les petits gâteaux aux amandes marocains.* Zuckersüß: Marokkanische Madelplätzchen. *Photo: Guy Hervais*

152 Arches and blossoms: courtyard of the Dar El Qadi hotel. *Arcs et fleurs : cour de l'hôtel Dar El Qadi.* Bögen und Blüten: Hof des Hotels Dar El Qadi. *Photo: Giulio Oriani/ Vega MG*

153 Refreshing aroma: a rose pool in Dar El Qadi. *Rafraîchissant et odorant : un bassin de roses au Dar El Qadi.* Erfrischend duftend: Ein Rosenbecken im Dar El Qadi. *Photo: Giulio Oriani/ Vega MG*

154 Still-life in orange: at Rita Kallerhoff's house in Marrakech. *Nature morte orangée : chez Rita Kallerhoff à Marrakech.* Stillleben in Orange: Bei Rita Kallerhoff in Marrakesch. *Photo: René Stoeltie*

156 Pretty shades: blue door at the CaravanSerai hotel. *Belles couleurs : porte peinte en bleu à l'hôtel CaravanSerai.* Schöne Töne: Blau gestrichene Tür im Hotel CaravanSerai. *Photo: Dorothea Resch*

157 Play of lights: at the pool of the CaravanSerai hotel. *Jeux de lumière : la piscine du CaravanSerai.* Lichterspiele: Am Pool des CaravanSerai. *Photo: Dorothea Resch*

158 Hovering artwork: colourful garden lantern. *Œuvre d'art flottant dans les airs : lanterne de jardin colorée.* Schwebendes Kunstwerk: Bunte Gartenlaterne. *Photo: Giulio Oriani/ Vega MG*

160 Sweet aroma: rose petals at the Amanjena hotel. *Un parfum délicat : pétales de roses à l'hôtel Amanjena.* Zart duftend: Rosenblätter im Hotel Amanjena. *Photo: René Stoeltie*

161 Carved: cedarwood door at the Amanjena hotel. *Joliment travaillée : porte en bois de cèdre à l'hôtel Amanjena.* Geschnitzt: Zedernholztür im Hotel Amanjena. *Photo: René Stoeltie*

162 Skylight: Elie Mouyal's bathroom in Marrakech. *Lumière zénithale : dans la salle de bains d'Elie Mouyal à Marrakech.* Oberlicht: Im Bad von Elie Mouyal in Marrakesch. *Photo: René Stoeltie*

164 Dream house for animals: birdcage at Rita Kallerhoff's house. *Maison de rêve pour les oiseaux : volière chez Rita Kallerhoff.* Traumhaus für Tiere: Vogelbauer bei Rita Kallerhoff. *Photo: René Stoeltie*

165 Colour circles: above a water tap at Rita Kallerhoff's house. *Cercles de couleur : au-dessus d'un robinet chez Rita Kallerhoff.* Farbkreise: Über einem Wasserhahn bei Rita Kallerhoff. *Photo: René Stoeltie*

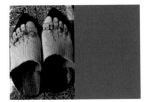

166 Trompe-l'œil: embroidered babuches from Fez. *Trompe-l'œil : babouches brodées de Fès.* Trompe-l'œil: Bestickte Babuschen aus Fes. *Photo: René Stoeltie*

168 Thousand reflections: at the Bled Targui near Marrakech. *Mille reflets de lumière : dans le bled Targui près de Marrakech.* Tausend Lichtreflexe: Im Bled Targui bei Marrakesch. *Photo: René Stoeltie*

169 Meditating at the fountain: quiet atmosphere in Bled Targui. *Méditer près de la fontaine : ambiance sereine au bled Targui.* Meditieren am Brunnen: Ruhige Atmosphäre im Bled Targui. *Photo: René Stoeltie*

170 Genuine handcraft: henna patterns. *Un véritable travail manuel : décorations au henné.* Echte Handarbeit: Verzierungen aus Henna. *Photo: René Stoeltie*

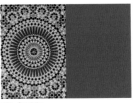

172 Take a seat: easy chair behind a highly decorative door. *Prenez place : fauteuil derrière une porte richement décorée.* Nehmen Sie Platz: Sessel hinter einer reich verzierten Tür. *Photo: René Stoeltie*

173 Silver and amber: prayer-beads in Frans Ankoné's house. *Argent et ambre : chapelet dans la maison de Frans Ankoné.* Aus Silber und Bernstein: Gebetskette im Haus von Frans Ankoné. *Photo: René Stoeltie*

174 Carefully restored: mosaic at the palace of the Glaoui. *Assemblée avec patience : mosaïque au palais de Glaoui.* Mühevoll zusammengesetzt: Mosaik im Palast des Glaoui. *Photo: René Stoeltie*

176 A big name: the Palais Jamaï hotel in Fez. *Un grand nom : l'hôtel Palais Jamaï à Fès.* Großer Name: Das Hotel Palais Jamaï in Fes. *Photo: Guy Hervais*

177 Much-loved ritual: mint tea in gold-rimmed glasses. *Rituel apprécié : servir le thé à la menthe dans des verres dorés.* Geliebtes Ritual: Minztee in goldverzierten Gläsern. *Photo: Guy Hervais*

178 Miniature pattern: at the Riad Enija in Marrakech. *Motifs en miniature : au Riad Enija à Marrakech.* Muster en miniature: Im Riad Enija in Marrakesch. *Photo: Reto Guntli*

180 Magnificent gate: handcraft at the Riad Enija. *Porte somptueuse : artisanat au Riad Enija.* Prachtvolle Pforte: Handwerkskunst im Riad Enija. *Photo: Reto Guntli*

181 Blue bathroom: relaxing in Riad Enija. *Salle de bains en bleu : détente au Riad Enija.* Bad in Blau: Entspannen im Riad Enija. *Photo: Reto Guntli*

182 Stone flowers: attractive wall decoration. *Comme des fleurs pétrifiées : jolie décoration murale.* Wie steinerne Blüten: Schöner Wandschmuck. *Photo: Gianni Basso/ Vega MG*

184 Flaming red: bedroom curtain at the Palais Ayadi. *Rouge flamboyant : le rideau de la chambre à coucher au Palais Ayadi.* Flammend rot: Schlafzimmervorhang im Palais Ayadi. *Photo: René Stoeltie*

185 Baroque-style shoes: at the Palais Ayadi. *Chaussures d'inspiration baroque : au Palais Ayadi.* Barock inspirierte Schuhe: Im Palais Ayadi. *Photo: René Stoeltie*

186 Substitute bell: ancient door-knocker in Marrakech. *Fait office de sonnette : heurtoir antique à Marrakech.* Statt Klingel: Antiker Türklopfer in Marrakesch. *Photo: Giulio Oriani/ Vega MG*

Addresses

AMANJENA
Route de Quarzazate, km 12
Marrakech
Morocco
Tel: +212 (44) 403 353
E-mail: amanjena@amanresorts.com
Website: www.amanresorts.com

CARAVANSERAI
264 Ouled Ben Rahmoun
Marrakech
Morocco
Tel: +212 (44) 300 302
E-mail: caravanserai@iam.net.ma
www.caravanserai.com

DAR EL QADI
79 Derb el Qadi
Azbest
Marrakech Médina
Morocco
Tel: + 212 (44) 378 061
E-mail: darelqadi@hotmail.com
www.darelqadi.com

DAR KAWA
102, Rue Dar el Bacha
Marrakech Médina
Morocco
Tel: +212 (44) 442 448

RIAD ENIJA
Rahba Lakdima
9 Derb Mesfioui
Marrakech
Morocco
Tel. +212 (44) 440 926
E-mail: riadenija@iam.net.ma
www.riadenija.com

PALAIS JAMAÏ
Bab el Guissa 30000
Fez
Morocco
Tel: + 212 (55) 634 331
E-mail: resa@palais-jamai.co.ma
www.palais-jamai.co.ma

Living in Morocco
Ed. Angelika Taschen / Barbara &
René Stoeltie / Hardcover, 280 pp. /
€ 19.99 / $ 29.99 / £ 14.99 /
¥ 3.900

Inside Africa
Ed. Angelika Taschen / Deidi von
Schaewen / Hardcover, 2 volumes,
912 pp. / € 99.99 / $ 125 /
£ 69.99 / ¥ 15.000

"In two volumes, this is a remarkable, colossal undertaking – more than simply a visual source book." —*House & Garden,* London, on *Inside Africa*

"Buy them all and add some pleasure to your life."

All-American Ads 40ˢ
Ed. Jim Heimann

All-American Ads 50ˢ
Ed. Jim Heimann

All-American Ads 60ˢ
Ed. Jim Heimann

Angels
Gilles Néret

Architecture Now!
Ed. Philip Jodidio

Art Now
Eds. Burkhard Riemschneider,
Uta Grosenick

Berlin Style
Ed. Angelika Taschen

Bizarro Postcards
Ed. Jim Heimann

California, Here I Come
Ed. Jim Heimann

50ˢ Cars
Ed. Jim Heimann

Chairs
Charlotte & Peter Fiell

Design of the 20ᵗʰ Century
Charlotte & Peter Fiell

Design for the 21ˢᵗ Century
Charlotte & Peter Fiell

Devils
Gilles Néret

Digital Beauties
Ed. Julius Wiedemann

Robert Doisneau
Ed. Jean-Claude Gautrand

East German Design
Ralf Ulrich / Photos: Ernst
Hedler

Eccentric Style
Ed. Angelika Taschen

Erotica 20ᵗʰ Century, Vol. I
From Rodin to Picasso
Gilles Néret

Erotica 20ᵗʰ Century, Vol. II
From Dali to Crumb
Gilles Néret

Future Perfect
Ed. Jim Heimann

HR Giger
HR Giger

Havana Style
Ed. Angelika Taschen

Homo Art
Gilles Néret

Hot Rods
Ed. Coco Shinomiya

Hula
Ed. Jim Heimann

India Bazaar
Samantha Harrison,
Bari Kumar

Industrial Design
Charlotte & Peter Fiell

Japanese Beauties
Ed. Alex Gross

Kitchen Kitsch
Ed. Jim Heimann

Krazy Kids' Food
Eds. Steve Roden,
Dan Goodsell

Las Vegas
Ed. Jim Heimann

London Style
Ed. Angelika Taschen

Mexicana
Ed. Jim Heimann

Morocco Style
Ed. Angelika Taschen

Native Americans
Edward S. Curtis
Ed. Hans Christian Adam

New York Style
Ed. Angelika Taschen

**Extra/Ordinary Objects,
Vol. I**
Ed. Colors Magazine

**Extra/Ordinary Objects,
Vol. II**
Ed. Colors Magazine

15ᵗʰ Century Paintings
Rose-Marie & Rainer Hagen

16ᵗʰ Century Paintings
Rose-Marie & Rainer Hagen

Paris-Hollywood
Serge Jacques
Ed. Gilles Néret

Paris Style
Ed. Angelika Taschen

Penguin
Frans Lanting

Photo Icons, Vol. I
Hans-Michael Koetzle

Photo Icons, Vol. II
Hans-Michael Koetzle

20ᵗʰ Century Photography
Museum Ludwig Cologne

Pin-Ups
Ed. Burkhard Riemschneider

Giovanni Battista Piranesi
Luigi Ficacci

Provence Style
Ed. Angelika Taschen

Pussycats
Gilles Néret

Seaside Style
Ed. Angelika Taschen

Albertus Seba. Butterflies
Irmgard Müsch

**Albertus Seba. Shells &
Corals**
Irmgard Müsch

See the World
Ed. Jim Heimann

Sneaker Book
Ed. Jim Heimann

Surfing
Ed. Jim Heimann

Sydney Style
Ed. Angelika Taschen

Tattoos
Ed. Henk Schiffmacher

Tiffany
Jacob Baal-Teshuva

Tuscany Style
Ed. Angelika Taschen

Women Artists
in the 20ᵗʰ and 21ˢᵗ Century
Ed. Uta Grosenick

ICONS